ALPHABET CITY

Stephen T. Johnson

PUFFIN BOOKS

To my parents,

for their constant belief in me and my art

The paintings for this book were created with
pastels, watercolors, gouache and charcoal
on hot pressed watercolor paper.

PUFFIN BOOKS
Published by the Penguin Group
Penguin Putnam Books for Young Readers, 345 Hudson Street, New York, NY 10014, U.S.A.
Penguin Books Ltd, 27 Wrights Lane, London W8 5TZ, England
Penguin Books Australia Ltd, Ringwood, Victoria, Australia
Penguin Books Canada Ltd, 10 Alcorn Avenue, Toronto, Ontario, Canada M4V 3B2
Penguin Books (N.Z.) Ltd, 182-190 Wairau Road, Auckland 10, New Zealand

Penguin Books Ltd, Registered Offices: Harmondsworth, Middlesex, England

First published in the United States of America by Viking, a division of Penguin Books USA Inc., 1995
Published by Puffin Books, a member of Penguin Putnam Books for Young Readers, 1999

39 40

THE LIBRARY OF CONGRESS HAS CATALOGED THE VIKING EDITION AS FOLLOWS:
Johnson, Stephen.
Alphabet City / by Stephen T. Johnson.
p. cm.
ISBN 0-670-85631-2 (hc.)
Summary: Paintings of objects in an urban setting present the letters of the alphabet.
1. English language—Alphabet—Juvenile literature. 2. City and town life—Juvenile literature.
[1. Alphabet.] I. Title.   PE1155.J645 1995 [E]—dc20 95-12335 CIP AC

Puffin Books ISBN:978-0-14-055904-0

Manufactured in China

Since childhood, I have been drawn to the particular energy one senses in the people, sounds, and structures, old and new, that constitute a city.

The idea for *Alphabet City* came to me while I was walking along a city street. I noticed an ornamental keystone that looked like the letter **S**. Then suddenly I saw the letter **A** in a construction sawhorse and the letter **Z** in fire-escapes. At that moment, it became clear that in urban compositions I could discover the elements that form the letters of the alphabet.

Building *Alphabet City* required self-imposed guide-lines. All letters had to be capital letters, found in their natural positions, out-of-doors or in public spaces such as the subway, readily accessible to anyone who looks carefully at our urban world at various times of day, and during the cycle of the seasons. There are no right or wrong solutions to finding letters in a city, only pleasurable ones. Some letters are obvious, while others, more subtle, come to light through a closer look.

I hope that my paintings will inspire children and adults to look at their surroundings in a fresh and playful way. In doing so they will discover for them-selves juxtaposition of scale, harmonies of shadows, rhythms, colorful patterns in surface textures, and joy in the most somber aspects of a city, by transcending the mundane and unearthing its hidden beauty.

S. T. J.